Walks in Dickens London: Victorian Camden Town

This walk explores Victorian Camden Town using the sketch map on the back cover. The area retains its 19th century atmosphere as a lively and scruffy mixture of Georgian terraced houses, and canal, railway and industrial survivals. Dickens lived here, aged around 10, when his family first slid into debt and neglected him. Many years later, when he had insisted on separating from her, his wife Catherine moved into a large house in the area. Scenes in *A Christmas Carol, David Copperfield, Dombey and Son* and *A Tale of Two Cities* return to the area.

Length: *Five miles; three hours.* ***Transport:*** *London Underground.*
Refreshments: *There are plenty of cafés, restaurants and public houses on the route.*
Places to sit in fine weather: *Churchyard of St Pancras Old Church, St Martin's Park, Oakley Square.*
Places to sit in wet weather: *See refreshments.*
Toilets: *The junction of Camden High Street and Camden Road, Camden Lock, the railway stations.*

Railways over London
by Gustave Doré from *London: A Pilgrimage* (1872)

Go to Kings Cross Station on the underground, and leave by the exit marked 'Pancras Road and British Library'. Walk west along the Euston Road, built as the New Road in the mid 18th century at the boundary of the city.

St Pancras Station is on your right. It was built on Agar Town, a badly drained shanty town. Dickens called it 'English suburban Connemara ... A complete bog of mud and filth with deep cart-ruts, wretched hovels, the doors blocked up with mud, heaps of ashes, oyster shells and decayed vegetables. The stench of a rainy morning is enough to knock down a bullock.' The people turned out of their homes when the site was cleared had to live in Central London, near their work, and crowded into other slums.

St Pancras Chambers
Photograph Sue Gane (2001)

At the end of the block is the entrance to **St Pancras Chambers**, built as the Midland Grand Hotel (1876) by Sir George Gilbert Scott. It is a masterpiece of neo-classical uniformity of decoration combined with picturesque irregular planning. The building was criticised when it first opened: 'There is here a complete travesty of noble associations, and not the slightest care to save these from sordid contact. An elaboration that might be suitable for a chapter-house, or a Cathedral choir, is used as an "advertising medium" for bag-men's bedrooms'. The hotel had lifts, known as ascending rooms, an imposing grand staircase, a long curved dining room and the first ladies' smoking room in London. It closed in 1935 and the building deteriorated It has been empty since the 1960s but was saved from demolition and given Grade I listed status as a building of exceptional architectural interest. The plan is to refurbish it as an international deluxe hotel.

Cross the busy Midland Road, turn right and walk north alongside the wall of the **British Library** (1997), which you will be able to visit at the end of the walk. (The British Library has exhibition rooms, a café and restaurant and toilets which are open to the public from 9.30 to 17.00 and 11.00 to 17.00 on Sundays. It is well worth a visit.) On your right you can see the curve of St Pancras Station's glass and iron train shed. It spans 240 ft, the widest in Britain, and is one of the wonders of Victorian engineering. The platform was raised on arches to 20 ft higher than Euston Road to allow the trains to cross the nearby Regent's Canal.

Take the first left into Brill Place and shortly afterwards turn right to walk through a small green park into Purchese Street. Turn right and walk north. The road, which changes its name to Goldington Street, has a complete terrace of mid 19th century houses on the west side, with pediments on the tall first floor windows. At the end you will find yourself in the elegant curve of Goldington Crescent. Directly opposite you across Pancras Road is the south wing of St Pancras Hospital (1889), its tall gaunt shape and central clock tower betraying its origin as the former St Pancras Workhouse. To the south of the hospital is a little gardener's cottage at the corner of the churchyard of **St Pancras Old Church**. Turn right, cross Pancras Road at the pedestrian crossing and enter the churchyard through the handsome black and gold wrought iron gates.

In *A Tale of Two Cities* Jerry Cruncher was a casual messenger for Tellson's Bank. 'Funerals had at all times a remarkable attraction for Mr Cruncher; he always pricked up his senses, and became excited, when a funeral passed Tellson's.' When a crowd approached 'bawling and hissing round a dingy hearse and dingy mourning coach' he was naturally interested to discover that the deceased was a police spy. The crowd deciding to escort the coffin 'to its destination amidst general rejoicing', Cruncher volunteered to ride in the mourning coach, modestly keeping out of sight from Tellson's. 'Its destination was the old church of St Pancras, far off in the fields.'

The Spy's Funeral
by H K Browne (Phiz) from *A Tale of Two Cities* (1859)

Cruncher 'made a short call upon his medical adviser – a distinguished surgeon – on his way back.' Late that night, having told his wife and son that he was going fishing, he left his home with 'a sack, a crowbar of convenient size, a rope and chain, and other fishing tackle of that nature'. Joined by two other fishermen and secretly followed by his son, Young Jerry, he walked north, climbed over an iron gate into a churchyard and 'fished with a spade, at first'. When Young Jerry saw the coffin emerge, and 'his honoured parent about to wrench it open' he fled home. (Cruncher supplemented his meagre earnings by digging up recently buried bodies in the dead of night, and selling them to doctors to use for dissection. Doctors were not allowed to use dead bodies to study anatomy with the exception, from 1540, of the corpses of executed criminals and, after 1832, of deceased workhouse inhabitants unclaimed by their next of kin.)

Inside the gate is a map showing the most interesting features of the churchyard. Walk up the steps to a large memorial sundial given by Angela Burdett-Coutts (1804-1906). As the heiress to the Coutts bank fortune, she was a very wealthy woman. She was a friend of Dickens, shared his concern for the poor and they worked together to remedy some of the evils. She also paid for the education of his eldest son Charley.

At the sundial turn right towards the church, the sole remaining fragment of medieval St Pancras. A Saxon altar of circa 600 has been found in the church, dating it as one of the earliest Christian sites in Europe. The present church was built in the mid 1300s but it was extended, restored and the tower added in 1848. The church is usually locked.

Go to the Hardy Tree beyond the east end of the church. The railway passes close to the church through what was once part of the graveyard. In 1865 the novelist Thomas Hardy (1840-1928), then apprenticed to an architect, had to supervise the job of exhuming bodies and dismantling tombs to make room for it. The headstones were set around this ash tree.

St Pancras Old Church
Photograph Sue Gane (2002)

At the tree turn left and walk to the elegant classical Soane Memorial, designed by the architect Sir John Soane for his wife who died in 1815. Just beyond the Soane Memorial is a large white box of a tombstone with a heavy growth of moss on its flattened pyramidical lid. This is the tomb of William Godwin and his first wife the early feminist Mary Wollenstonecraft Godwin (1759-97), who wrote *A Vindication of the Rights of Women* in 1792. In 1814 her daughter Mary (the author of *Frankenstein*) and the poet Percy Bysshe Shelley confessed their love over this gravestone.

Leave the graveyard by the nearby east gate, descend the stairs into Camley Street and turn left. From the 1760s this area was covered in dust heaps and Dickens set *Our Mutual Friend* amongst them. John Harmon, a miser, 'grew rich as a Dust Contractor, and lived in a hollow in a hilly country entirely composed of Dust. On his own small estate the growling old vagabond threw up his own mountain range, like an old volcano, and its geological formation was Dust. Coal-dust, vegetable-dust, bone-dust, crockery dust, rough dust and sifted dust, - all manner of Dust.' The 'dust' included human and animal excrement. It was sifted and sorted by hand, as shown in the picture on the opposite page, and 'Golden Dustmen' like Harmon made fortunes from selling it to brickmakers, or as manure to the market gardens that surrounded the city. Camley Street is close to the Regents Canal, so it was easy and cheap to transport useable waste.

View of a Dust Yard from *London Labour and the London Poor* by Henry Mayhew (1861)

Continue walking north up Camley Street until you reach the bridge over the Regents Canal, descend the stairs to the towpath and turn right. The canal was completed in 1820, linking the Docks at Limehouse to the Grand Union Canal, which links London and Birmingham, at Paddington. It carried coal, building materials, fodder and refuse and continued in use until the docks closed in the 1960s. Pass under the first bridge by the Constitution public house. This carries St Pancras Way, one of London's ancient roads that wound along beside the River Fleet. The Fleet rises on Hampstead Heath and joins the Thames at Blackfriars; it is now in a culvert and used as a sewer. Climb the stairs at the second bridge and turn left and immediately left again.

You are now in Royal College Street, named after the Royal Veterinary College, Camden Town. The area was known for its fields of cows until the end of the 18th century when Lord Camden granted leases to build 1,400 houses. An ambitious plan was prepared with a linked crescent and oval, but building was disrupted when the Euston railway line was built through it in 1830. The canal attracted industry and the area became the unfashionable and remained that way for over 100 years. Gentrification began in the 1960s.

Cross Royal College Street at the traffic lights and walk down Georgiana Street. Pause at Lyme Street to look at the remnants of a piano-making factory (1855) on the west side. (Camden Town was a centre of piano-making in the 19th century.) It has a four-storey pedimented middle bay and is flanked by slightly earlier houses.

Cross Camden Street and walk into the small park called St Martin's Gardens. As London grew the small churchyards beside the city's parish churches started to overflow. The churches bought land for burial grounds in the surrounding fields. St

Martin's Gardens was formerly the burial ground of St Martin-in-the-Fields in Trafalgar Square. In the mid 19th century the churchwardens tried to sell the burial ground for building, but local people rioted, stoning the builder's workmen and it was laid out as a public garden.

Follow the park to the left and leave by the gate into Pratt Street. Turn right, walk to the traffic-ridden Bayham Street, turn right again and walk north past, on your right behind a tall privet hedge, the almshouses of St Martin-in-the-Fields (1818). The yellow-brick building with red surrounds to its windows on the opposite side of the road at the junction with Greenland Road was built in 1910 as the Hampstead and North London hospital. A plaque on the building marks the site of **No 16 Bayham Street** where the young Dickens lived with his parents in 1822-5. At the time Camden Town was quiet, respectable and semi-rural; residents had to walk to work. But John Dickens, a clerk in the Navy Pay Office, was in debt, he did not send his ten-year-old son to school and Dickens felt neglected.

Marley's Ghost by John Leech from *A Christmas Carol* (1843)

He described 16 Bayham Street as 'a mean small tenement, with a wretched little back-garden abutting on a squalid court'. It had four rooms, a basement and a garret and housed Mr and Mrs Dickens, their five children, a servant and a lodger. Dickens used houses like 16 Bayham Street several times in his fiction.

In *A Christmas Carol* Bob Cratchit worked as clerk to the wealthy but miserly Scrooge. He earned 15s a week, three quarters of the poverty-line wage for a family. Like John Dickens, he lived with his wife and five children in a four-roomed house in Camden Town. Scrooge raised Cratchit's salary after the ghost of his dead partner Marley appeared to him and arranged for three other ghosts to remind him of the true Christmas spirit.

In *David Copperfield*, Tommy Traddles lodged with the Micawbers in a little street in Camden Town. The house had 'an indescribable character of faded gentility' and an angry milkman outside 'because that there little bill has been running so long, that I begin to believe it's run away altogether, and never won't be heerd of.'

Continue up Bayham Street to the junction with Camden Road and turn right. On the opposite side of the road is St Michael's Church (1890s), deliberately urban with big flying buttresses in imitation of a 14th century Friars Church. It is difficult to get inside the church but the interior is said to be impressive with a very high ceiling.

Next door to St Michael's is Sainsbury's (1988) by Nicholas Grimshaw, 'all grey like an aircraft hangar and revelling in its dour engineering image. It was Grimshaw's first supermarket, and one of the first to demonstrate that such a building can have not only architectural quality but an urban form.'

Sainsbury's Camden Town
Photograph Sue Gane (2002)

Cross at the pedestrian crossing, enter Sainsbury's and walk straight through to the car park and take the first exit into Kentish Town Road. (The store is open most of the time, but if it is closed turn left and walk down Camden Road to the junction with Kentish Town Road.)

Turn right and walk up Kentish Town Road, cross at the pedestrian-controlled lights and turn left down Hawley Crescent beside Elephant House, a red brick former brewery backing onto the canal. Continue walking west past another grey metal hangar-type building with a futuristic curved façade, built as television studios (TVAM) in 1982. When you reach Camden High Street cross at the traffic lights and turn right. This is the centre of Camden Town, a lively mixture of shabby Georgian terraces and survivals of 19th century industrial buildings. Large papier-mâché models decorate the modest houses above market stall style shops selling fashionable clothing. It is very busy at weekends.

At the bridge over the Regent's Canal turn left into the precinct of the castellated and stuccoed early 19th century lock-keeper's cottage, now an information centre and café. **Camden Lock** has twin lock chambers side by side, built to save water since one lock could be emptied into the other. The canal is crossed by a brick road bridge (1820s) and a cast iron pedestrian bridge (1854) with an 80 ft span and a tiered arch design, built for a man to lead one of the horses that drew the barges across the canal.

Camden Lock (photograph Sue Gane, 2002)

Cross the canal by the pedestrian bridge. Ahead on your left the Ice House is being converted into apartments. It was built to hold ice, imported from Norway until the 1900s, in large brick cylinders up to 100 ft deep. Nearby is Gilbey's elegant white gin distilling and bottling works (1894). On your right an old railway warehouse (1905) has a water tower for fire fighting. This area is now Camden Lock market, with cobbled yards and buildings filled with specialist craft shops and stalls and plenty of cafés.

Continue west to the next bridge, where you can see the Birmingham railway line (which reached Euston Station in 1837) crossing the canal in front of you. Ascend the stairs opposite the modern castellated Pirate Club and turn right into Oval Road. At the junction with Gloucester Crescent you will see a striking round building, built as a piano factory in 1852. The pianos were hoisted down a central well. Walk down Gloucester Crescent and pause at Inverness Street, in the centre of the crescent. Ahead of you are typical late Victorian substantial Italianate houses, built in pairs for the wealthier middle classes, along curving roads and with plenty of room for servants.

Gloucester Crescent (photograph Sue Gane, 2002)

In 1858 Dickens separated from his wife Catherine, after 22 years of marriage and the birth of ten children. (Dickens had met and fallen in love with a young actress, Ellen Ternan, the previous year.) Catherine went to live in Gloucester Crescent, initially with her oldest son Charles, but later alone. Her sister Georgina Hogarth stayed with Dickens in the role of housekeeper.

Catherine saw her children occasionally but she was not allowed to attend her daughter wedding in 1860. Kate said, 'My father was a wicked man - a very wicked man .... My father was not a gentleman - he was too mixed to be a gentleman ...My father did not understand women .... he was not a good man, but he was not a fast man, but he was wonderful! ... We were *all* very wicked not to take her part; Harry does not take this view, but he was only a boy at the time, and does not realise the grief it was to our mother, after having all her children, to go away and leave us. My mother never rebuked me. I never saw her in a temper. We like to think of our geniuses as great characters - but we can't.'

Women in a children's hospital
by Gustave Doré from *London: A Pilgrimage* (1872)

The Doré engraving shows women as Victorians liked to see them: young, pretty and visiting sick children. This sort of sex stereotyping underpinned Dickens' treatment of his wife. He was very sensitive about any criticism of his behaviour and fell out with Miss Burdett-Coutts when, at Catherine's request, she tried to mediate between the couple. Dickens also ceased his long association with Phiz because he illustrated a magazine published by a friend with whom he had quarrelled over the separation.

Turn left into Inverness Street and take the first right into Arlington Road. The bulky red brick building with turreted corners (No 220) is Rowton House (1905), one of a number of men's lodging houses built by Lord Rowton. Walk south down Arlington Road crossing Parkway and Delancey Street. Note the alleyways into Camden High Street on your left and the complete stucco trimmed terraces on your right. Turn right into Mornington Street and left into Mornington Terrace beside the railway line.

In *Dombey and Son* the Toodle family lived in Staggs's Gardens, in Camden Town, known to its inhabitants as Camberling Town. It 'was a little row of houses, with little squalid patches of ground before them, fenced off with old doors, barrel staves, scraps of tarpaulin, and dead bushes; with bottomless tin kettles and exhausted iron fenders, thrust into the gaps. ... The first shock of a great earthquake had, just at that period, rent the whole neighbourhood to its centre. Traces of its course were visible on every side.

Houses were knocked down; streets broken through and stopped; deep pits and trenches dug in the ground; enormous heaps of earth and clay thrown up; buildings that were undermined and shaking, propped by great beams of wood. Here, a chaos of carts, overthrown and jumbled together, lay topsy-turvy at the bottom of a steep unnatural hill; there, confused treasures of iron soaked and rusted in something that had accidentally become a pond. Everywhere were bridges that led nowhere; thoroughfares that were wholly impassable; Babel towers of chimneys, wanting half their height; temporary wooden houses and enclosures in the most unlikely situations; carcases of ragged tenements and fragments of unfinished walls. ... In short, the yet unfinished and unopened Railroad was in progress; and, from the very core of all this dire disorder, trailed smoothly away, upon its mighty course of civilisation and improvement.'

The Toodle Family in Camden Town
by Phiz from *Dombey and Son* (1848)

But six years later, 'there was no such place as Staggs's Gardens. It had vanished from the earth. Where the old rotten summer-houses once had stood, palaces now reared their heads, and granite columns of gigantic girth opened a vista to the railway world beyond. The miserable waste ground, where the refuse-matter had been heaped of yore, was swallowed up and gone. The old by-streets now swarmed with passengers and vehicles of every kind; the new streets that had stopped disheartened in the mud and waggon-ruts, formed towns within themselves.' The Toodles had moved and the directions to their new home seem to take you back to Bayham Street.

Continue to the end and turn right into Mornington Crescent (1832). This is an attractive terrace with pretty iron balconies, spoiled by the large 1920s tobacco factory, built in what would once have been communal gardens. In 1905 the painter Walter Sickert (1860-1942) lived at number 6, marked with a blue plaque. He was a British Impressionist and leader of the Camden Town group of painters who rented studios and lodgings in the then robustly working class area.

Sickert rented studios at No 247 Hampstead Road, part of the site of the **Wellington House Academy** where Dickens was a pupil for two years after his father had been released from the debtor's prison. He left at age 15 to earn his living as a lawyer's clerk. The school was demolished when the railway line was built: 'Locomotives now run smoothly over its ashes'. Dickens was happy there and his fellow pupils saw him as the 'son of a gentleman'.

Turn around and walk north to Mornington Crescent Underground Station. Cross Eversholt Street and walk east along the busy Crowndale Road, originally a medieval track leading to St Pancras Church. The **Working Men's College** (1906) is on your left, in a neo-Georgian style. The hall at the east end has a curved wall and the symmetrical classroom block has a central pediment crowned by a white wooden cupola. The college was started by the Christian Socialist F D Maurice in 1854, the first British adult education college, aiming to offer first class education to working men. The writer John Ruskin and the painter Dante Gabriel Rossetti taught there.

Cross to the east side of Oakley Square, which has gardens which are open to the public and is a pleasant place to rest on a fine day. Turn right and at the first opportunity turn left to cut through the apartment block to Chalton Street in Somers Town. The Dickens family lived here (at 29 Johnson Street – no longer there) when Dickens attended the Wellington House Academy. Turn right and walk south down Chalton Street.

Somers Town was built in the 1790s around a fifteen-sided polygon of 32 outward facing houses each three stories high. But the market crashed 'and many carcasses of houses were sold for less than the value of materials'. The area became shabby, home to the working classes and French émigrés fleeing the French Revolution. Dickens lodged in the Polygon for a few weeks in 1824. Mary Wollenstonecraft lived with her husband at No 29. The Polygon was demolished in 1890.

Mr Skimpole (at the piano)
By Phiz from *Bleak House* (1852)

In *Bleak House* Mr Skimpole 'lived in a place called the Polygon, in Somers Town. Whether he was a better tenant than one might have supposed, in consequence of his friend Somebody always paying his rent at last, or whether his inaptitude for business rendered it particularly difficult to turn him out, I don't know; but he had occupied the same house some years. It was in a state of dilapidation quite equal to our expectation. Two of three of the area railings were gone; the water-butt was broken; the knocker was loose; the bell-handle had been pulled off a long time, to judge from the rusty state of the wire; and dirty footprints on the steps were the only signs of its being inhabited.'

Continue in Chalton Street crossing Phoenix Road and turning right through a narrow alleyway into Churchway. In Dickens's time this narrow lane was crowded with poor housing. On the corner of Grafton Place are some of the earliest low-income apartments, in an attractive Arts and Crafts style varied by a broken frontage. Cross Euston Road at the traffic lights to **St Pancras New Church**.

St Pancras New Church was built in 1822 when London became built up to the south of the New Road. It replaced St Pancras Old Church, too far away and too small, as the parish church. It was the most expensive church of its time, designed by the Inwoods in a classical style with a portico of six fluted Ionic columns stretching the entire width of the church. On either side are two small pavilions, copies of the portico of the caryatids of the Erechtheum and the tower copies the Grecian Tower of the Four Winds. It is worth going into the church if it is open. It has galleries on lotus columns, a flat ceiling and charming stained glass windows of the early 1880s.

From the church return to Euston Road and turn right. Note the Fire Station on your left on the corner of Eversholt Street, an outstanding example of the free Arts and Crafts style, with a lively asymmetrical façade and pretty irregular domestic windows. Pause to admire the view of the red and grey Gothic towers of St Pancras Chambers behind the matching red-brick modern rectangular blocks of the British Library. Continue east along Euston Road to return to Kings Cross Station, the end of the walk.

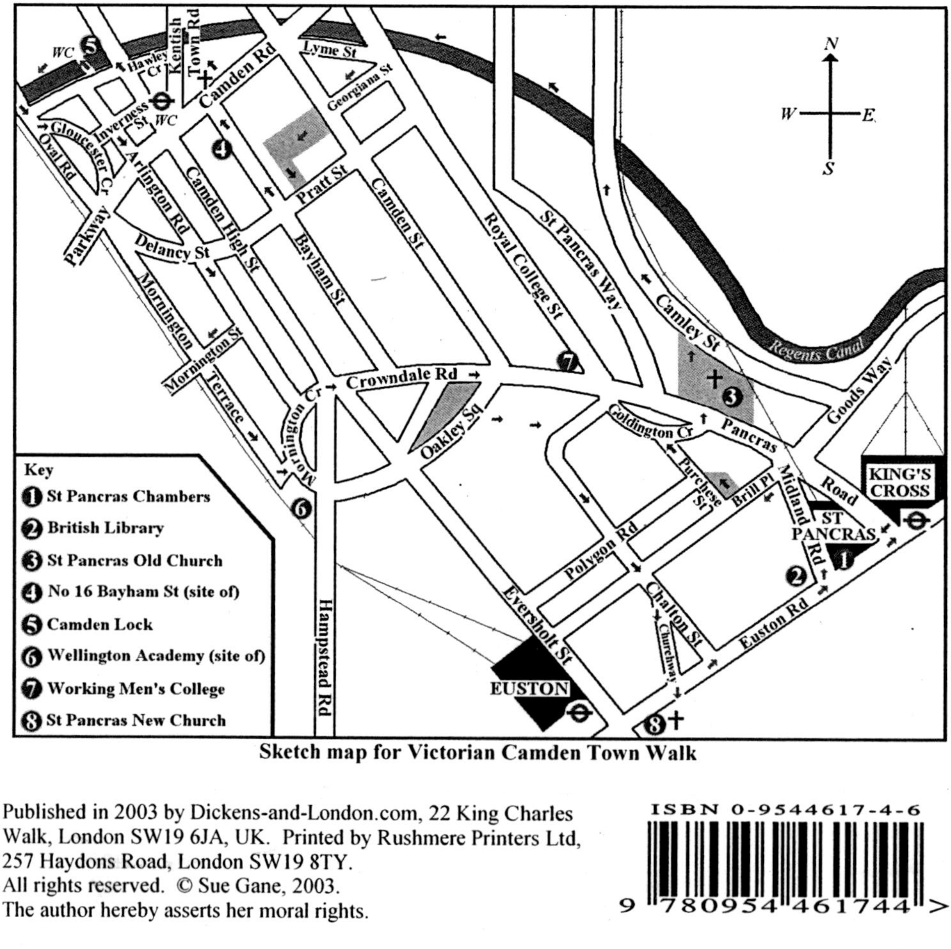

Sketch map for Victorian Camden Town Walk

Published in 2003 by Dickens-and-London.com, 22 King Charles Walk, London SW19 6JA, UK. Printed by Rushmere Printers Ltd, 257 Haydons Road, London SW19 8TY.

ISBN 0-9544617-4-6
9 780954 461744